TOBIAS PICKER

My Name is Agnes

from *Fantastic Mr. Fox*

for Mezzo-Soprano and Piano

Schott Helicon Music Corporation

ED 30092

Tobias Picker
b.1954

My Name is Agnes
from *Fantastic Mr. Fox*

for Mezzo-Soprano and Piano

Libretto by Donald Sturrock
Based on a story by Roald Dahl

ED 30092

www.schott-music.com

Mainz · London · Madrid · New York · Paris · Prague · Tokyo · Toronto

My Name is Agnes

from "Fantastic Mr. Fox"

Donald Sturrock

Tobias Picker

So don't mess____ with me, guys!____ Do you get what I mean?

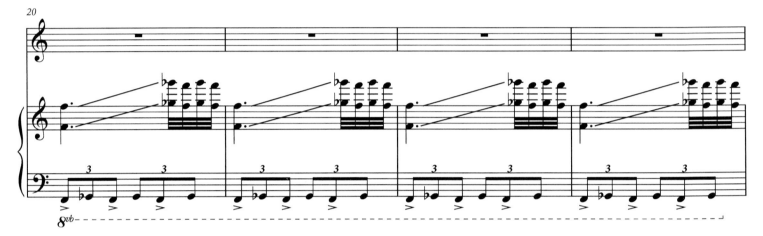

My jaws are mag-nif-i-cent, dead - ly and dark. My teeth are____ as vi - cious

____ and sharp as____ a shark's. If I grind 'em at you, there are sure to be sparks! So don't mess with this

moth-er of ma-tri-archs! _____

To dig is to dev-as-tate, crush and de-stroy.

To de-mol-ish and bull-doze_____ gives me such pure joy, that dig-ging's my on-ly de-sire and de-

light. And I long to an-ni-hi-late all day and night!_____

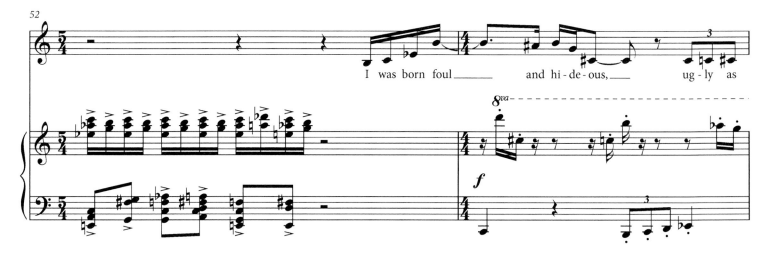

I was born foul_____ and hi-de-ous,_____ ug-ly as

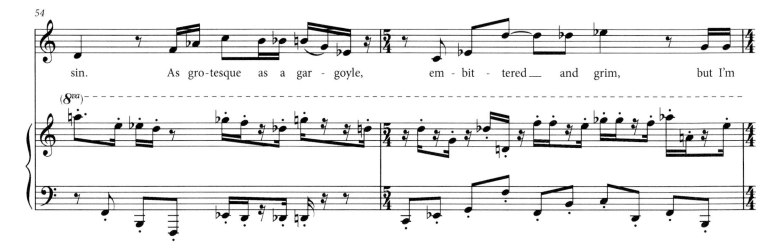

sin. As gro-tesque as a gar - goyle, em - bit - tered___ and grim, but I'm

strong as a li - on and fierce as a friend, I'm an en - gine of ter - ror, I'm a kill - ing ma - chine!___

To dig is to dev-as-tate, crush and de-stroy. To de-mol-ish and bull-doze

_____ gives me such pure joy, that dig-ging's my on - ly de-sire and de-

light. And I long to an - ni - hi -late all day and night!_____ DIG!

DIG! DIG!

Schott Helicon Music Corporation

254 West 31st Street, 15th Floor
New York, NY 10001
Tel: 212 461 6940
Fax: 212 810 4565
ny@schott-music.com

ISBN-13: 978-1-4803-4446-4

Distributed By

HL 49019584
ISBN: 978-1-48034-446-4

TOBIAS PICKER

Dove Aria

from *Thérèse Raquin*

for Mezzo-Soprano and Piano

SCHOTT

Schott Helicon Music Corporation

ED 30093